Business

With

Guts

SENTON KAÇANIKU

Copyright © 2023 Senton Kaçaniku

All rights reserved.

ISBN: 9798861329521

DEDICATION

This book, "Business with Guts", is dedicated to the brave, daydreaming risk-takers - the mavericks who dare to march to the pace of their own drum and undertake uncharted terrains with fervor and zealous determination. This recognition extends to all the budding entrepreneurs and the unnoticed outliers, who have tirelessly burned the midnight oil to turn their visions into reality.

May these pages serve as a tribute, to you, the fearless warriors of commerce who fight against conventional rules and methods, unafraid of taking the road less traveled. You who envision opportunities where others only perceive risk, brave enough to place your faith in the power of innovation and future-forward thinking, rather than limiting yourself to the timeworn pathways of success.

To the unflinching women entrepreneurs, who have broken the glass ceiling again and again in the world of business. May this book celebrate your audacious spirit, your endless resilience, and your unyielding tenacity; empowering women across islands and continents to smarm the world of business with your grace, grit, and gumption.

This work is also an ode to young dreamers whose minds are brimming with ideas as immense as the cosmos. Your bold visions and audacious plans reassure us that our future is in innovative and daring hands, capable of taking giant strides and leaving lasting footprints on the sands of time.

To the underdogs and the contemporaries, whose bravery, imagination, and industry breathe life into their concepts, making them tangible, viable businesses that continuously shape and redefine the world we live in. May you find solace, encouragement, and the spark of boldness in these chapters as you stride forward on your entrepreneurial journey.

To the self-starters and lone sailors who refuse to wait for the winds of chance but unfurl their sails and charter their route across the vast expanses of the business landscape, uninhibited by adversity, discouragement, or fear. Your bold spirit and the courage that propels you to reject defeat, fight through despair, and rise, time and again, is the heart of this book.

Just as the lionhearted pioneers of industry have blazed trails before us, lighting the path with their audacious determination and dogged endurance, may this book serve as a beacon, illuminating your way to business success and wealth. For you, it is a testament that fortune indeed favours the bold, a narrative of men and women whom audacity has turned into legends, and a guide to help you forge your path ahead.

May "Business with Guts" breathe life into your dreams, bolster your courage, and bolster the spark that ignites the fire of entrepreneurship within you. This book is an emphatic salute to your undying spirit, a testament to your iron will, and a hearty vote of confidence in your unflinching bravery.

Here's to you – the bold, the brave, the visionaries. This book is for you, and may you find within its pages the courage to dream bigger, aim higher, and strike harder till you turn your dreams into reality!

With unwavering faith in your abilities and boundless admiration for your unwavering spirit, this book, "Business with Guts," is dedicated.

CONTENTS

	Acknowledgments	i
	Introduction: The Bold Path of Entrepreneurship	1
1	Boldness and Confidence	6
2	The Power of Vision: Creating a Bold and Compelling Future	12
3	Building a Winning Team: The Art of Leadership and Inspiration	19
4	The Importance of Sales and Marketing: Boldly Connecting with Your Audience	26
5	Managing Finances and Cash Flow: Bold Strategies for Financial Mastery	33
6	Scaling Your Business: Boldly Expanding Your Reach and Impact	38
7	Navigating Challenges and Setbacks: Boldly Overcoming Obstacles	64
8	Innovation and Creativity in Business: Boldly Shaping the Future with Visionary Ideas	84
9	Building a Sustainable Business: Boldly Making a Difference for Generations to Come	100
10	Leading with Purpose - Boldly Creating a Legacy That Matters	106
	Conclusion	112

ACKNOWLEDGEMENTS

First and foremost, I extend my deepest gratitude to the tenacious entrepreneurs who allowed me access into their world of high-stakes risk, relentless determination, and pioneering spirit. This book, "Business with Guts", would not exist without their willingness to openly and candidly share their unforgettable journeys in the often tumultuous waters of entrepreneurship.

My sincere appreciation goes to all the brilliant men and women who were bold enough to take risks, inspiring the very theme of this book. Their stories are a testament to the power of courage, resilience, and an unabashed belief in one's vision. They are the true embodiments of what it means to conduct 'Business with Guts'.

A very special note of gratitude to my indefatigable

editor, whose unwavering support and precise editing contributed immensely towards shaping this project into the cohesive, insightful piece it is today. Her keen eye and immense patience were essential throughout this journey of writing about the world of business.

On a more personal level, I can't forget to acknowledge my family, whose constant encouragement provided me with the strength to devote time, energy, and heart into this demanding project. They were my rock through the sleepless nights, never-ending edits, and stages of self-doubt.

Last but certainly not least, I would like to express my sincere gratitude to you, the reader. Your interest in 'Business with Guts' and the cutthroat, exhilarating world of fearless entrepreneurship is the reason why I wrote this book. My utmost aspiration is that it proves to be a helpful guide to your own journey towards business success, encouraging you to be bold, take risks, and pursue wealth in your own way.

Before I wrap up these acknowledgements, let me acknowledge one last entity: failure. It might seem strange, but my profound gratitude goes to every setback, obstacle, and so-called 'failure' I've encountered in this journey. These experiences taught me to stick to the grind, to maintain resilience even when things get uncomfortable and, essentially, to do business with guts.

'Business with Guts' began as a distant dream, an ambitious vision. Today, with great gratitude, I hold it in my hands as a reality, standing by to inspire the risk-takers and visionaries of tomorrow's business world.

INTRODUCTION: THE BOLD PATH OF ENTREPRENEURSHIP

Entrepreneurship is not for the faint of heart. It takes guts, courage, and a willingness to take bold risks. But for those who are willing to embrace this bold path, the rewards can be enormous.

"Business with Guts" is a comprehensive guide to entrepreneurship, written by Senton Kacaniku. In this book, you will discover the power of boldness and confidence, the art of leadership and inspiration, and the strategies for financial mastery that can help you create a thriving business that makes a difference in the world.

From individuals just beginning with an inkling of an idea, to established business giants looking to innovate and evolve, this book is designed to provoke the challenge and fruit of daring audacity in business. Welcome to "Business with Guts", a guide to encourage entrepreneurs to brazenly chase their dreams, take audacious risks, and attain an unprecedented realm of success and wealth.

On this journey, you will be confronted not by faint-hearted suggestions, but by the vivid reality of bold business. We will dive head-first into domains where only the brave venture, exploring concepts that define not just good, but great entrepreneurs. So fasten your mind's seatbelt as we venture down this exciting path less journeyed, a path that promises the breath-taking rollercoaster that is entrepreneurship.

Chapter 1 spotlights an essential ingredient in a world where mediocrity is a dime a dozen - boldness and confidence. We delve into the psychology of courage in business, revealing how this ingredient can make or break an enterprise.

Chapter 2 throws light on the immeasurable Power of Vision, helping you to etch out an audacious and compelling future.

Chapter 3 navigates into the arena of leadership and inspiration and how crucial it is in assembling a winning team.

Chapter 4 showcases the significance of dripping boldness into your sales and marketing strategies, thus forming unshakable bonds with your audience.

Chapter 5 uncovers strategies to become a maestro in managing finances and cash flow - the lifeblood of your bold venture.

Chapter 6 raises the curtain on the overwhelming yet rewarding challenge of scaling your business, offering you strategies that expand your reach and deepen your impact.

Chapter 7 rallies you to equip with the courage to overcome challenges and setbacks, teaching you the art of turning naysayers into motivators.

Chapter 8 calls your spirit to harness innovation and creativity in business, thus shaping your future with visionary ideas.

Chapter 9 engages your mind in establishing a sustainable business - a venture that defies time and continues to make a difference.

Chapter 10 finally inspires you to lead with purpose, creating a legacy worth remembering, a legacy that matters.

This book will not only introduce you to taking bold steps in the entrepreneurial world, but it will also challenge you to balance that boldness with calculated risks, a focused vision, and a passionate persistence. Here, we believe in Business with Guts, and we invite you to join us on this incredible journey to make your bold and audacious dreams a reality, and in doing so, leaving an invaluable and unforgettable mark in the business world.

Let's get started. May your journey be brave and your rewards be bold. Remember - fortune indeed favors the bold. Welcome to Business with Guts!.

1 BOLDNESS AND CONFIDENCE

Part 1: The Psychology of Boldness

Boldness is the quality of being fearless and daring, of taking risks and embracing uncertainty. It is the willingness to step outside of your comfort zone and to do what others are afraid to do. To understand the psychology of boldness, we must first define what we mean by the term.

Boldness is not just a personality trait; it is also a learned behavior. You can cultivate boldness by taking small risks and gradually building your confidence. Each time you take a risk and succeed, your brain releases dopamine, a chemical that reinforces the behavior and makes you feel good.

But why is boldness important in entrepreneurship? Simply put, because entrepreneurship is all about taking risks. Whether it's launching a new product, entering a new market, or making a strategic investment, every decision you make as an entrepreneur involves some degree of risk.

Part 2: The Science of Confidence

Confidence is another key quality of successful entrepreneurs. It is the belief in yourself and your abilities, and the ability to stay calm and focused in the face of adversity. Confidence is not just a feeling; it is also a physiological state.

When you feel confident, your brain releases cortisol, a hormone that helps you stay alert and focused. It also suppresses the production of adrenaline, which can lead to anxiety and stress. But how can you cultivate confidence as an entrepreneur?

One of the best ways is to set achievable goals and focus on your strengths. By setting small goals and achieving them, you can build your confidence and develop a positive feedback loop. Confidence also comes from experience, so the more experience you gain as an entrepreneur, the more confident you will become.

In the second half of this chapter, we will provide practical tips and techniques for developing your boldness and confidence, so that you can take your business to the next level.

Part 3: Practical Tips for Developing Boldness and Confidence

Now that we have a better understanding of the psychology and science behind boldness and confidence, let's explore some practical tips and techniques for developing these qualities as an entrepreneur:

Take calculated risks: To cultivate boldness, start by taking calculated risks. Identify potential risks and rewards, and weigh the pros and cons before making a decision. Start with small risks and gradually work your way up to bigger ones.

Learn from failure: Failure is a natural part of entrepreneurship, and it can actually be a valuable learning experience. When you experience failure, don't dwell on it. Instead, reflect on what you can learn from the experience and use it to improve your future decisions.

Surround yourself with positive people: The people you surround yourself with can have a big impact on your confidence and mindset. Surround yourself with positive, supportive people who believe in your vision and encourage you to take risks.

Practice mindfulness: Mindfulness is the practice of being present in the moment and fully engaged in your surroundings. By practicing mindfulness, you can develop a sense of calm and clarity that can help you make better decisions and stay focused on your goals.

Celebrate small victories: Celebrate your small victories along the way, such as reaching a milestone or achieving a goal. This can help build your confidence and reinforce the behaviors that lead to success.

By following these tips and techniques, you can develop the boldness and confidence necessary to succeed as an entrepreneur. In the following chapters, we will explore other important qualities of successful entrepreneurs, and provide practical advice and real-world examples to help you achieve your business goals.

2 THE POWER OF VISION: CREATING A BOLD AND COMPELLING FUTURE

Picture this: You are standing at the base of the mighty Everest, peering through the misty cloud cover that engulfs the immortal giant. The peak appears distant and unattainable, but deep down in your heart, you know that the sheer power of your will to conquer, your courage to dream big, can lead you to claim victory upon the icy precipice. Welcome to the world of bold entrepreneurs!

Being an entrepreneur is essentially setting yourself up on this ascent - the uncompromisingly treacherous and intimidating rise to Summit of Success. But before you affix your harness and lock your pickaxe into the frozen mountain, you must possess an impeccably unwavering Vision.

Throughout history, visionaries have shaped our world, pushing the boundaries of human understanding, engineering society's progress. The likes of Jeff Bezos, Elon Musk, and Steve Jobs didn't allow their thinking to be constricted by the box of conventionality. They nurtured vivid visions, taking erratic leaps and defying gravity of the conventional mindset. By breathing life into their dreams, they moulded our reality, thereby inscribing their names into the annals of business legends.

The binary composition of vision – clarity and audacity – breathes life into the field of dreams. Excavate your aspirations from within, and endow them with the boldness of mind as you illustrate a lucid pathway leading towards them. Your vision is not a variable, susceptible to be influenced by external factors. It is an axiom, standing resilient amid storms of doubt and negativity, becoming the catalyst for your entrepreneurial conquest.

Visions are the blueprints of your business empire. They sketch the contours of tomorrow and plant seeds that grow into towering edifices. However, be warned: creating a vision requires audacity and tenacity in equal measures. You need to have the gall to map out a grand strategy and the resilience to stick to it amidst turbulence of uncertainties.

Behind every successful venture, there is a

daring vision. For Jeff Bezos, the vision was to build the most customer-centric company in the world. Today, Amazon stands as a testament to his audacious dream. Also, Elon Musk's SpaceX, borne out of the bold vision of making space travel accessible, felt like an audacious daydream. Yet, today, it's ferrying astronauts to and from the International Space Station.

So, how does one create a compelling vision? Begin by answering what problem your venture solves, who it serves, and most importantly, why it's crucial. The answer should prompt action that reinvigorates the ties between your aspirations and the world's needs. Surely, this demands esoteric introspection and ruthless focus, but the reward is the generation of a clear, compelling vision that wildly motivates the entrepreneur within.

Following inspiration, comes the arduous task of actualization. Once your vision paints a boldly inviting future, goals bridge the chasm between vision and reality. Set short-term, mid-term, and long-term goals. As you knock each one of them down, you step closer to your grand vision. The satisfaction of achieving small wins parlay into the fortitude to tackle next vision-aligned goal, ushering a cycle of success.

However, remember the wisdom sewn in limitations, for only the sky isn't one. The temptation to veer away from your path is a Siren call you must resist. The vision beckons you, and it's your responsibility to align your decisions, invest your time and resources wisely to maintain congruence with the vision.

Bear witness: Creating your vision isn't a flippant wish or lazy daydream. It's a challenging yet thrilling journey that requires courage, adaptability, grit, and yes, Guts. Driven by your vision, guided by goals, and backed by smart decisions and relentless efforts, your business will soar- reaching the pinnacle where risks become opportunities, setbacks transform into rallying points, and audacious dreams morph into reality.

Thus, take a moment now to visualize your business aspirations. Breathe life into your wildest dreams, shaping them into a compelling vision that propels you and your team towards success. As you tread the path of entrepreneurship, powered by an insatiable desire to innovate, let your vision be your light, illuminating your path into the misty future.

Remember, your vision is the soul of your entrepreneurial endeavor. Nurture it. Not as something useful for a once tweeted company motto or as mere words on an ignored office plaque, but as the spirit that ignites your pursuit. Bold entrepreneurs are visionaries, fearless dreamers who dare to see beyond the horizon, who flaunt colossal ambition. Equip yourself with a vision that dares, dreams, and perseveres, and the world of entrepreneurship will not remain unchartered.

Indeed, this is the Business with Guts. This is the realm where audacious dreams meet the grit, turning the impossible into the possible, charting a bold and compelling future. Converge your ambition with action, and you'll carve your place in the einherjar of business heroes. So, gear up for an exhilarating adventure. Let your dreams soar. After all, no Everest was ever climbed with feet on the ground. Embrace the fear, fuel your vision with eagerness and brace yourself for a rollercoaster ride shadowed with risks, lit by rewards. You are an entrepreneur. You are a visionary.

Own your Vision. Own your Business with Guts.

3 BUILDING A WINNING TEAM: THE ART OF LEADERSHIP AND INSPIRATION

Fish rots from the head down. Such isn't merely an old saying; it's a business truth. Business success and wealth creation begin with leaders who inspire their teams to be bold, take risks, and step outside comfort zones. But how can an entrepreneur become such a leader? This journey is a continuum; it never ends.

Leadership is not a role but a state of mind. Traditionally, we used to think of a leader as the person at the top, the individual with a whip, commanding the workforce. But in a world that celebrates innovation, where the landscape is constantly evolving, we need a new leadership paradigm. Today's business world doesn't need bosses; it needs leaders—visionaries who create a compelling picture of the future, who inspire their teams to climb their Everest.

In this chapter, we'll look at the skills you'll need to fire up your team and inspire them to take the bold steps necessary for your business to surge ahead.

1. Creating a Vision

Casting a vision is the very foundation of leadership. As the captain of the ship, you are the one who sets the course. Where are we going? What's the grand plan? Your vision should be compelling and big enough to bootstrap employees out of their comfort zones. You are not just selling products or services, and you are selling dreams—dreams of a better future.

The missionaries win over the mercenaries in the march of time. People get fired about a cause, a mission that resonates with them. Get your team excited about where the company is headed. Drive them with the big picture, inspire them with possibilities. Your vision should be like a magnet, pulling all towards a common goal.

2. Building Trust

Without trust, even the most compelling vision

will fall flat. The bricks to a great building project are laid with trust. Your team should believe in you and trust your decisions. This trust isn't bestowed; it's earned. As a leader, you need to cultivate openness, honesty, and transparency.

Make your word your bond. Stand by your commitments. Show up for your team. Admit when you are wrong. Involve them in decision-making processes, hear out their suggestions, value their contribution, and give credit where it is due.

3. Empowering Success

A company is only as good as its team. You may have the most revolutionary idea, but without a great team behind it, success will be but fleeting. Real leaders create an environment where their team can succeed.

Your employees are not workhorses, but assets. Empower them with the right tools, the right mindsets, support their learning and development. Encourage risk-taking and do not punish mistakes, but instead, see them as opportunities for learning and growth.

4. Leading by Example

Actions speak louder than words. People will believe what they see more than what they hear. As a leader, demonstrate your commitment to your vision by walking your talk. Embody the traits that you wish your team to have. Workers will emulate what they see rather than what they hear.

5. Embracing Change

In the world of business, the only constant is

change. Leaders who resist change are like dinosaurs – secondary to extinction. Embrace change, and inspire your team to do the same. Encourage creativity and innovation. Storms may come, but with a leader who navigates with fortitude and flexibility, the team will sail on, undeterred.

6. Keeping it Human

Emotionally intelligent leaders understand that their team is made up of humans, not robots. People have emotions, desires, strengths, and weaknesses. Recognize and celebrate success, empathize during setbacks, and always, maintain an atmosphere of respect and dignity.

Leadership is a journey, not a destination. It's about growth, learning, and change. It's about becoming the inspiration for your team, pushing them past mediocrity to the edges of their potential. It's not about control; it's about empowerment. True leadership is the art of turning a vision into a mission, driving it with unyielding passion, and inspiring followers to become fellow visionaries in the quest.

Remember, bold businesses need bold leaders. And bold leaders create bold teams. Embrace the art of leadership and start building your winning team today. Only then can you truly conduct business with guts.

4 THE IMPORTANCE OF SALES AND MARKETING: BOLDLY CONNECTING WITH YOUR AUDIENCE

Sales and marketing, the heartbeats of a thriving business, are two spheres that demand courage and boldness. This chapter will underscore the critical role of these two elements in accomplishing your entrepreneurial dream.

Traditionally, sales and marketing have been seen as separate entities within a business operation. Marketing is the artful strategy on creating awareness, arousing interest, and creating the desire for a product or service. Sales, on the other hand, captures the essence of driving the final transaction, turning prospects into paying customers. A bold entrepreneur understands the importance of these two functions for business growth, profitability, and sustainability.

Boldness is essential in sales and marketing. The marketplace is often hazardous terrain with cut-throat competition and ever-changing consumer dynamics. Fierce competition triggers stagnancy, driving businesses into obscurity.

However, bold individuals welcome these challenges and use them to refine their sales and marketing strategies, positioning themselves strategically in the business playing field. Bold entrepreneurs understand that embracing bold and audacious sales and marketing strategies is not an option, but a fundamental rule for survival and growth.

Your marketing strategy should be designed to steeply differentiate your product or service in a crowded marketplace. This daring differentiation begins by understanding your audience. Without insight into their needs, preferences, and pain points, any marketing communication or sales effort will miss the target. Bold entrepreneurship involves deep diving into customer psychographics, making sense of data intelligently and using this information as fuel to drive your marketing and sales engine.

Personalization should be central to your marketing strategy. Today's customers value a business that understands their unique needs and caters to them. They crave bespoke experiences, personalized messages, and tailor-made solutions. These aspects establish a deep connection with the audience, fostering trust and loyalty, which are paramount in closing sales.

Aggressive creativity in marketing is synonymous with boldness. Conventional marketing strategies offer safety, but it stifles the opportunity to be daring, disruptive, and memorable. A fearless marketing campaign leaves a lasting impression by speaking directly to the heart of potential customers. It doesn't shy away from eliciting strong emotions, sparking debates, or even being polarizing. This powerful emotional connection drives customer engagement, and when leveraged correctly, transforms into sales.

Now, let's switch lanes to sales. The bold entrepreneur understands that sales is not just about money changing hands, but rather relationship-building. Your sales strategy should be more about fostering connections, less about transactions. Harnessing the power of human nature, curiosity, and the desire for value to persuade prospects to become paying customers is the key to sales success.

Negotiation is a central component of sales. A bold entrepreneur knows that negotiations require courage, emotional intelligence, and mental resilience. Navigating the murky waters of price negotiations, dealing with objections, and convincing customers of the value of your product or service can make even the most hardened business professional uncomfortable. However, a successful entrepreneur pushes past this discomfort, adopting a confident and assertive stance that ultimately chalks up in the success column.

Customer relationships don't end once the cash

register rings. Bold entrepreneurs understand that the customer journey is cyclical, not linear. They continuously engage customers with insightful content, appreciation messages, and responsive customer service. These relationship-fostering strategies nourish customer loyalty, fostering repeat business and recommendations, which are significantly cheaper means of generating sales compared to acquiring new customers.

In conclusion, neither a great product nor a noble business idea has ever sold itself. It takes the bravery of venturing into the realm of bold sales and marketing strategies to turn prospects into satisfied customers. This chapter urges you to bravely embrace the challenge; harness the tools available, grasp the nuances of your audience, speak to them fearlessly, negotiate unabashedly, and commit to the ongoing relationship with the vivacity needed for a thriving business. Be daring, be memorable. Your audacity in sales and marketing is the key to unlock the doors of unprecedented business success.

Remember, it's your 'Business with Guts' that will make you dominate the marketplace. And bold sales and marketing strategies are the sinews of that courage.

5 MANAGING FINANCES AND CASH FLOW: BOLD STRATEGIES FOR FINANCIAL MASTERY

Financial management can seem daunting, especially when it pertains to running a business. The trick lies not in the amount of money but how intelligently it's deployed. It's not about being cautious but being bold. It's about taking calculated risks and maximizing opportunities.

Everyone thinks about making money. But few venture into the daring realm of managing it strategically: the realm of 'Business with Guts.'

With that said, financial management does not necessitate recklessness. 'Bold' does not equate 'rash'. As an entrepreneur, you must balance daring and discretion. This chapter provides you a roadmap to navigate through these complexities as if you were born for it.

Firstly, let's talk about the pivotal aspect of financial planning - cash flow management. Every business, irrespective of its size or age, lives and dies by its cash flow. As the old adage goes, "Cash is king." Bold entrepreneurs, however, don't just rely on cash alone; they use it as their scepter, directing it where to flow, mold, and grow.

Sustaining positive cash flow is an art that demands innovative strategies. One such strategy is to negotiate better terms with suppliers. Most entrepreneurs overlook the power of negotiation out of sheer reluctance. Dispatch this reluctance and bargain for extended payment terms. This bold move will keep your cash within your business for a longer period and makes funds available for operational uses and potential investments.

Another strategy concerns accounts receivable – many businesses operate on the basis of credit. However, unpaid invoices can strangle your cash flow. Dare to defy the norm and put dynamic strategies into practice such as incentives for early payments or penalties for late payments. By doing so, you not only exercise control over when you'll receive payment, but you also keep your debtors alert and respectful of your terms.

Next, let's jump into the concept of financial leveraging. Leveraging is where the audacity and acumen of a true entrepreneur are truly tested. It's a term that excites some and terrifies others; simply put, it's the use of borrowed funds to boost potential returns. This needs to be handled deftly. Success in leveraging lies in carefully choosing ventures that provide higher returns than the interest payable, thus amplifying net profits.

Lastly, indulge in the shrewd movement of funds. Dare to explore high-return investment opportunities, diversify to spread risk, and pump funds back into your business to fuel growth. Strive to strike a balance between low-risk, low-returns safety nets, and high-risk, high-returns ventures. This is the crux of a bold, yet strategic financial management approach, it's a daring dance on the tightrope of risk and return.

Furthermore, don't shy away from seeking professional advice. The world's most successful entrepreneurs aren't those who know everything, but those who know when to seek help. Engaging financial advisors, chartered accountants, or investment professionals can provide valuable insights and keep you from financial pitfalls.

In summary, the best way to manage your finances and cash flow is akin to playing chess. You can't win by playing safe; you have to take daring yet calculated steps. Evaluate every decision with a keen eye, from a shift in cash flow to investment opportunities.

Financial mastery is not about shrinking away from risks, but embracing them with consideration. As an entrepreneur, you need not just a wallet, but wisdom to thrive in the market jungle.

So, brace up and master your finances and cash flow like a boss with a bold heart, a keen mind, and, most importantly, with guts. For it is only the

'Business with Guts' that breaks barriers to build fortunes.

6 SCALING YOUR BUSINESS: BOLDLY EXPANDING YOUR REACH AND IMPACT

Recognizing you have made a successful dent in your marketplace is a rewarding milestone. However, within the game of business, standing still is the same as moving backward. As the bold entrepreneur, you must opt to expand. And this process, known as business scaling, requires nothing short of courage and audacity.

To scale a business, you have to connect the different aspects of the entrepreneurial venture. This entails boldly pushing beyond comfort zones, taking on more significant challenges, making bigger investments, and possibly enduring more significant setbacks. And yes, you could potentially earn larger profits.

So how exactly does an entrepreneur make such a move? How do they go from the standard field to playing at a global level? Here's a step-by-step guide to take you through the scaling process.

Step 1: Build a Solid Base

The first step in boldly scaling your business is akin to building a grand architectural masterpiece - you need to lay down a solid and resilient foundation that can withstand the weight of massive future growth. This means that before embarking on the journey of expansion, you must first meticulously examine, and reinforce your existing operations – your base. Here's how to go about it:

1. Operational Stability: Just as a strong and well-erected structure can withstand pressure and the elements, a stable operational structure is the backbone of a scalable business. Establishing the right operational foundation includes creating systems that are efficient and processes that are easily repeatable. Keep refining them to handle more workload, and to mitigate the challenges accompanying upscaling.

2. A Loyal Customer Base: Customers are your business's lifeblood – they contribute to its wellbeing, growth, and sustainability. Therefore, nurturing a base of loyal customers is indispensable. Win them over not only with high-quality product offerings but also with exceptional customer service. A satisfied and loyal customer base acts as the keystone, strengthening your business's foundation.

3. A Strong, Vision-aligned Team: Integrating a high-performing team into your business is crucial. Hire people who share your business's vision and values, and cultivate a mutual understanding and collaboration within the team. The synergy created bolsters the core operational structure, and the cultivation of a resilient internal culture fuels sustainable growth.

4. Insight and Learning: As a business leader, one of your ongoing tasks should be to develop a deep understanding of your industry, your competitors, market trends, and your operations. Be committed to learning from your own successes and failures, as well as those of others in your space. Reflect on these lessons to adjust your strategies. This knowledge and wisdom will form an integral part of your solid base – your business acumen.

5. Risk Management: A well-prepared entrepreneur understands that risk is synonymous with business. It's crucial to identify risks in your business operations and devise strategies to manage them effectively—Plan for contingencies and cultivate a proactive problem-solving mindset in your team.

In essence, creating a solid foundation for your business before scaling is about playing to your strengths while minimizing weaknesses. It's about working within known factors and refining them to perfection. By building this base, you are paving the path for successful scaling – one that's robust and can support ambitious growth without breaking. Now that you have laid down the groundwork, you are ready to propel into the vast expanse of scaling opportunities.

Step 2: Market Analysis

Insights drawn from market analysis serve as the compass for navigating your business expansion paths. Start by scrutinizing your target market penetration and identifying your penetration percentage. Consider the potential customers you've not yet reached, and sketch a plan for targeting them.

Expand your purview beyond client number; try to understand their preferences, needs, and behaviors. What are the latest market trends that relate to your product or service? How can they offer pointers for reinventing your offerings? For instance, a trend toward eco-friendly products could usher a line of green alternatives of your merchandise. Keep a constant eye on these trends, whether they are directly connected to your field or tangentially. Remember, trends can be temporary, but identifying them early on provides a competitive advantage.

Next, draw a bead on the patterns forming in your market space. These patterns could be seasonal, demographic, or geographic. Analyzing such patterns will help with strategic decision-making about introducing new products, services, or campaigns at the right time and the right place.

Proceed to potential prospects. Is there untapped potential in your existing market, or is there another market waiting to be discovered? For instance, if you're in a B2B business, consider if your product might also suit B2C or vice versa. Explore potential overseas markets, as well.

This brings us to identifying gaps. During expansion, it's crucial to pinpoint the chinks in your armor to fortify your position. Is there something your competitors do differently and better? Could your business improve customer service or product packaging? Does your marketing strategy need an upgrade? Besides internal gaps, seek gaps in the market - needs, desires, or worries of consumers not being catered to effectively. Your ability to fill that gap could seal your success.

All this information sums up into a comprehensive market analysis, painting an accurate picture of where your business stands and where it ought to head. The key to successful market analysis lies in constant vigilance and flexibility, accommodating changes to your strategies as needed. It's grounded in the willingness to see things as they are, not as we wish them to be.

In the end, a detailed market analysis serves as

your roadmap, charting your course through uncharted territories during your business expansion journey. Building your business with guts demands that you confront and utilize the complex realities of your market landscape – it's a tough task, but remember, the rewards are as sizeable as the risks. In the next part, we will delve into how exactly you can turn the insights gathered from market analysis into actual business strategies. So dig in. Steel yourself. Plot your course. After all, fortune favors the brave.

Step 3: Innovate Boldly

Innovation is the lifeblood of any business, particularly so for those seeking to scale. It's in the very spirit of innovation where audacity finds a home, and through its expression, businesses can truly transcend their current limitations and form a robust path toward scaling.

The interplay between innovation and scaling is a dance of risk and reward. Innovation is inherently risky - it demands moving beyond proven methodologies and venturing into uncharted territories. Scaling, equally, calls for embracing the unknown, expanding your operations, and accepting the challenges that come with it. Both require an unwavering will and the audacity to make daring decisions.

Key to embracing innovation is daring to be different. You must strive to set your business apart from the crowd and the competitors. This uniqueness is not just about being conspicuous - it's about developing a compelling value proposition that resonates with evolving customer needs and shifts the parameters of competition. This might involve altering your business strategies, production processes, product designs, or delivery mechanisms, all in a bid to infuse novelty into your operations.

Staying one step ahead of the game is another fundamental principle here. As a scaling business, your eyes should be set on the future, predicting and preparing for what's next. Incorporating futuristic vision into your business strategy, spotting market trends, and integrating them into your initiatives helps establish a dynamic and robust enterprise model. Utilizing advanced technologies or adopting green practices are classic examples of this preemptive approach.

Innovation should also extend to the way you engage with your customers. As their needs evolve, so should your strategies to fulfill them. Remain acutely aware of consumer trends, market demand, and ever-fluctuating sentiments. Adapt your service offerings, develop new products based on customers' requirements, or modify your business procedures, all in line with improved consumer experiences.

Relentless pursuit of fresh ideas serves as fuel for the engine of scaling. This involves continuously searching for innovative strategies, whether through meticulous research, brainstorming sessions, or scanning the global business landscape for inspiration. Every aspect of your company, from the business model to product offerings, from customer service strategies to marketing paradigms, should be open to examination and rejuvenation.

Being innovative may require overhauling well-established business models or operational systems, but don't let familiarity breed inertia. It's a task not for the faint-hearted, but for the audacious – those who possess not just the courage to dream, but the will to transform these dreams into reality.

In essence, when we talk about 'Business with Guts,' innovation lies at the very heart of it. It's about mustering the courage to disrupt, the resilience to endure the journey, and the audacity to continuously reach out for the novel, untried, and untested. It's what provides the momentum for making an impact significantly larger than what you started with, scaling up your enterprise, and ultimately, bolstering your reach.

Step 4: Embrace Technology

Embracing technology stands as a critical step in scaling any business in today's digital age. Without integrating the use of technology, companies risk being left behind in an ever-evolving marketplace.

When we talk about embracing technology, we're suggesting that you use digital tools for streamlining operations, creating efficient internal systems, and adjusting to the evolving business landscape.

Technology is significant in numerous ways. One, it allows businesses to manage deeper and broader complexities as they scale. It provides innovative solutions for handling larger volumes of work, which is critical when scaling. Can your current system manage double or even triple its present load efficiently and without cracking under pressure? If you fear it might not, integrating robust technological systems can assuage such concerns and assist in handling larger volumes without glitches.

Additionally, as an entrepreneur looking to scale, you must appreciate the role of technology in speed and efficient service delivery. In the fast-paced business world, expedited service delivery can be a game-changer. Technology facilitates instant communication, hastens process times, ensures faster delivery of products, and improves service delivery. In its absence, your business might just be the slow elephant amongst fast-moving gazelles.

The third point to note about technology is its contribution to achieving higher accuracy in business operations. Navigating a larger market, risk increases, hence your processes require a high degree of precision. Come in big data analytics and cloud-based systems. These tools enhance accuracy in monitoring business trends, making projections, understanding your customer base, including financial management. When these details are clearly and accurately noted, then anticipating the growth trajectory becomes more precise, thus ensuring you're scaling correctly.

Progressive businesses also harness the power of technology for marketing purposes. Digital marketing tactics have proven time and again to be incredibly effective in reaching wider audiences, engaging potential clients, and turning them into loyal customers. Advanced SEO strategies, social media advertising, email marketing, content development–these tech-based marketing strategies have the power to thrust your business in front of millions globally.

Lastly, entrepreneurs embarking on a scaling journey must adopt technological advancements for their innovative potential. In this dynamic era, staying ahead of the competition involves offering innovative products and services. Unleash your creativity utilizing state-of-the-art technology to establish ground-breaking offerings, separating your brand from the crowd.

In conclusion, embracing technology demonstrates your audacity as an entrepreneur ready for the future of commerce and your commitment to providing optimal services to your customers. The key message here is: integrate technology, embrace its benefits, and navigate the pitfalls to leverage its full potential as you daringly scale up your venture.

Step 5: Strategic Partnerships and Collaborations

One of the most efficient ways to scale up is forming strategic partnerships and collaborations. As the famous African proverb says, "If you want to go fast, go alone. If you want to go far, go together." This phrase particularly holds true in the business landscape. When done strategically, alliances can propel your business to unimaginable heights.

Concept of Partnerships

At its core, a strategic partnership entails a collaboration between two or more businesses with the aim of achieving mutual growth. Businesses come together, pooling resources, knowledge, and expertise, creating a synergy that benefits every party involved. These alliances can be formed between businesses within the same industry (non-competitors) or across different sectors.

Benefits of Partnerships

One of the primary benefits of partnerships is the influx of fresh ideas. Each participant brings their unique perspective, novel techniques, and innovative problem-solving tactics, cultivating a fertile ground for creativity and growth. You benefit from the thought capital, experiences, and innovative prowess of all involved.

An extended customer base is another advantage. When companies partner, they expose themselves to each other's customers, promoting cross-advertising and co-branding opportunities. This can lead to increased brand visibility, higher lead generation, and subsequently, improved sales.

Partnerships also allow access to diversified distribution channels. A company with product 'A' might have a robust online presence but struggles with physical outlets. At the same time, a company with product 'B' may have an extensive network of physical stores and outlets but lacks a solid online presence. In such a case, a partnership could bridge these gaps, allowing both companies to leverage each other's strengths.

The Audacious Approach

Venturing into partnerships and collaborations

demands boldness. It necessitates you stepping out of your comfort zone to establish beneficial connections. Investigate potential partners, assess mutual compatibility, and project potential growth trajectories.

Preparation is key when making the first contact. Show potential partners how desirable your business is as a collaborator. Showcase your strengths, demonstrate your value proposition, and express your vision for a progressive future together.

While proposing any partnership, it's essential to maintain transparency. Discussing the terms explicitly will ensure everyone is on the same page, preventing future disagreements.

A Word of Caution

While alliances can be profoundly beneficial, ensuring they bear fruit requires due diligence. Ensure your potential partner shares the same values, has a harmonious corporate culture, and is financially stable. Analyzing such factors before any formal agreement will protect you from potential disappointments or losses.

Remember, forming a strategic partnership isn't about capitalizing on the resources of another company; it's about creating a win-win situation. Be not only courageous in seeking partnerships but also wise enough to make the right choices.

In conclusion, scaling a business requires more than just capital and a robust customer base. It calls for bold and strategic partnerships. These alliances can fast-track your growth, making your dreams of expanding your business a closer reality.

Step 6: Learning from Mistakes

Courage, as they say, is not the absence of fear. It is having fear and choosing to act nonetheless. Within the scaling journey, this courage comes in the boldness to take risks, to step into unchartered territories, knowing fully well that the risk of failure looms. Risk and failure are intertwined within the fabric of business. Recognizing that they can tumble the best of plans is a critical part of your growth process as an entrepreneur.

Acceptance is the first step towards learning from your mistakes. Accept that you will make missteps and encounter roadblocks along your scaling journey. These setbacks are inevitable components of your business's evolution. Embrace them instead of fearing them. Understand that you are not alone; businesses of all sizes encounter similar growing pains. Assigned the wrong person to a crucial role? Made a poor investment?

Launched a product before its time? All these are lessons cloaked in the cloak of mistakes.

Once accepted, your duty is to understand the lesson each setback teaches. Analyze what went wrong, where, and how. This introspection can provide invaluable insights that you may have missed within the bustle of scaling. Understand that this is not an exercise in self-punishment, but a method to avoid repeating the same mistake. Lessons well learned translate into fewer repeats of failures, saving you time, resources, and heartache in the future.

Failure, though painful, is a potent fuel for perseverance. It has a sting sharp enough to ignite your resolve to reach for success with renewed vigor. Use your errors as motivation to improve and perfect your models, systems, and strategies. Ask yourself each time, "How can I do better?". Channel the negative energy of failure into a driving force that propels your business forward.

The process of learning from mistakes is transformative. From operational methods to strategic decisions, these lessons will reshape your business and you as an entrepreneur. And remember, every failure is not an endpoint but a bend in the road. While it may throw you off path, it also offers an opportunity to redirect your journey towards a potentially better route. In essence, each failure is merely a stepping stone - a tough, hard, jagged stepping stone - but each serving as a stepping stone towards sustainable growth and ultimate success.

Being an entrepreneur means being comfortable with discomfort. It implies developing a relationship with your failures and learning how you can dance with them instead of against them. After all, in business and in life, it's less about avoiding mistakes and more about learning, growing, and expanding from them. The most successful entrepreneurs are those who fail, learn, grow, and persist, for they understand that progress, though sometimes born of failures, is a product of persistence and courage. It is always the next step beyond the setback. Don't fear the failures, be expectant of the growth they bring. Embrace the falls, but always anticipate the rise that comes after.

Now that you are armored with the acceptance of inevitable setbacks and the knowledge of how to leverage them, it's time to map out the expansion of your business boldly and courageously.

Parting Words

Scaling signifies the transition from being a player inside the business arena to becoming the game changer. It's about manifesting your full potential - for profit, for impact, for a legacy. When you decide to scale, realize that it's not just about size. It's about reach, it's about influence, it's all about making your mark.

In a nutshell, scaling a business requires "Business with Guts." It requires a blend of testicular fortitude, strategic acumen, innovative audacity, and relentless ambition. There will be countless obstacles, but pushing past them will define your true success as a risk-taking, profit-making, limit-defying entrepreneur.

As you finish this chapter, it's time for a swift reality check. Are you ready to give your business the expansion it's itching for? Are you ready to take up the challenge? Are you ready to show the world your brand's true potential? Then let us proceed to the next level, where we introduce growth strategies that would help you make bold moves within the marketplace. You're ready, I can tell.

7 NAVIGATING CHALLENGES AND SETBACKS: BOLDLY OVERCOMING OBSTACLES

The trail of an entrepreneur's journey may not always be a flat, smooth road. There are bumps, detours, dead-ends, and hundred-foot walls that seem impossible to overcome. This chapter will shed light on the art of overcoming obstacles, turning challenges into opportunities and setbacks into comebacks—a flame only found in the heart of those who dare to do business with guts.

A setback is nothing but the setup for a comeback. It's a phrase that holds a weight of importance for anyone seeking success and wealth in the business world. The first step to overcoming challenges is to see them not as insurmountable obstacles but as opportunities for growth.

The Proactive Mindset

Diving into the complex world of entrepreneurship, effectively navigating this labyrinth requires a robust, defensive yet equally offensive weapon - your mindset. A mindset doesn't simply handle the way you perceive the world, every decision you make, every action you take, every judgement call in your business strategy stems from it. The mindset which entrepreneurs found as their undefeated champion is the proactive mindset.

Granted, the term might seem overused, a cliché in the world of self-growth guides. But the proactive mindset is beyond a mere buzzword. It's a practical model of thinking that can eradicate obstacles and pave the way to success.

Now, let's analyze the essence of a proactive mindset by comparing it to its polar opposite - the reactive mindset. Imagine a sudden problem arising within your business – a major client pulls out last minute, leaving a gaping hole in your financial projections. A reactive individual, in such a situation, will likely be swept up in the chaos. They might freeze, panic or make hasty decisions in a desperate attempt to 'put out the fire.' The unexpected problem becomes a major roadblock, inducing stress and possibly leading to more poor decisions.

Flip that on its head, and you have the proactive entrepreneur. This person foresees potential complexities and prepares for them. They take preventive measures, always one to two steps ahead. They have Plan As, Plan Bs, and even Plan Cs. They acknowledge that problems will arise but refuse to be entrapped by them. Instead of seeing challenges as catastrophic, they see them as intellectual puzzles waiting to be solved, or better yet, opportunities for growth and learning.

To them, the sudden departure of a major client is not a disaster but a challenge with its respective solution. They may have anticipated and prepared for such a scenario by diversifying their client base, implementing risk mitigation strategies, or preparing contingency plans. They don't waste time and energy worrying or being taken aback; instead, they take calculated actions towards a solution. They may even seek to turn the situation into an opportunity to bring in new clients or pivot towards more profitable avenues.

The proactive entrepreneur knows that problems, challenges, and setbacks are a package deal with success. But they refuse to let these keep them in a stranglehold. They understand that how they react to these challenges determines the success or failure of their enterprise.

But how do you change your mindset from reactive to proactive? It's about embracing the challenges you'll face on your journey. It's about constant learning, refining strategies, remaining unfazed, and always be ready to take the initiative. Accept the fact that you are in control of your actions and reactions and let this belief guide your journey towards becoming an entrepreneur ready and equipped to do "Business with Guts".

Reframe the Situation

In the rugged landscape of entrepreneurship, one of the most powerful tools you can harness is your perspective. Elite entrepreneurs have mastered the power of reframing—a cognitive behavioral technique that involves changing the light in which you view a situation to manipulate the emotional fallout from it. It's not about insulating yourself from the realities or sugar-coating the hard facts, rather, it's a way to reset your mental compass to navigate through the storm.

As a business juggernaut, you're bound to encounter financial turbulence. Revenues may be wilting, debts might be piling up causing the cash-flow to resemble more of a trickle. You could go the conventional way of viewing this as a setback - an anchor pulling your dream venture down into the abyss of failure. But is that viewpoint going to solve your predicament? Probably not.

Instead, try reframing your situation. Look at it from a different perspective. Perhaps this financial trouble, as troubling as it seems, is an opportunity in disguise. Could it be a prompt to make your operations more lean and efficient? Is it a harsh, yet effective reminder that your budgeting skills need honing? Maybe, this is your chance to identify and shed any financial dead weight, thus making your business leaner and meaner.

Alternatively, could it possibly be the push you require to think outside the box and uncover new revenue streams? Diversifying your income can not only act as a contingency plan but also unveil new market opportunities that you were previously blind to.

Reframing is not an act of overnight metamorphosis, it's a habit cultivated by throwing yourself into the deep end repeatedly with the faith that you'll come up swimming. Gradually, as you cultivate this habit, you notice that these so-called obstacles lose their formidable facades, revealing what they truly are - detours leading onto untrodden paths.

Nonetheless, making this shift in your mindset is no easy feat. It requires large doses of self-awareness, mindfulness, and patience. With each successful reframe, you'll notice your ability to bounce back gets stronger, your business acumen sharper and your overall grit tougher.

In conclusion, as you refine your mindset, you're not just overcoming hurdles but weaving a safety net that will catch you when you fall, bounce you back on your feet, and propel you further into success. Indeed, operating a business with true boldness requires a willingness to look adversity right in the face and still see an opportunity—this is the essence of reframing!

Prepare for the Unexpected – Scenario Planning

Many great victories in business have been owed not only to a confident, problem-solving mindset but equally to the implementation of foresight and expert planning. With a future as unpredictable as it is unwritten, achieving success requires you to hone the skill of preparing for the unexpected through scenario planning.

Scenario planning involves defining a set of different futures or scenarios and assessing how your business could respond in each instance. It's a strategic exercise that goes beyond straight-line prediction. It is about anticipating various 'what if' outcomes, both optimistic and pessimistic, and preparing an arsenal of effective responses.

Think of scenario planning as creating a roadmap for the journey to your entrepreneurial dreams, one that encompasses multiple routes. You will chart these potential courses of action, visualizing different landscapes, obstacles, and avenues. It's akin to playing a strategic game of chess, thinking multiple moves ahead, and creating a plan B, C, and even D.

More importantly, scenario planning allows you to x-ray your business, allowing you to scrutinize your strengths, weaknesses, opportunities, and threats — a SWOT on steroids. By identifying these factors, you learn to play into your strengths, shore up weaknesses, capitalize on opportunities, and guard against threats. You lay foundations for a robust decision-making framework that is data-informed and future-proof.

Scenario planning also helps to build resilience in the face of uncertainty. It enables you to identify key trigger points, factors that will cause significant shifts in your business landscape. By monitoring these triggers, you are positioned not only to react but to take action before the shifts disrupt your business.

Furthermore, scenario planning stretches your strategic thinking abilities. When you consistently engage in considering multiple possibilities, you develop the cognitive flexibility to adapt to shifting landscapes. This exercise can also stimulate creative problem-solving, prompting you to think outside the box and devise innovative solutions for complex challenges.

However, the key to successful scenario planning is to regularly revisit and revise your plans. The future is fluid, and the scenarios you envisage today may no longer be valid tomorrow. Continually reassessing your strategies to adapt to new information and changes in your business environment is critical.

In conclusion, scenario planning is an invaluable tool for any businessperson looking to navigate the turbulent waters of entrepreneurship. It fosters a proactive and resilient approach to managing challenges and prepares you to face unexpected events with boldness and confidence. It is not just about predicting what may come but preparing your business to withstand, adapt, and triumph over anything that comes your way.

Leverage Resources and Networks

It is a common fallacy to believe that entrepreneurship equates to solitary traveling. Contrarily, the entrepreneur's journey is packed with opportunities to connect, learn, and grow together. Resources and networks are like the compass and map in your entrepreneurial expedition, ready to guide when the paths seem twisted and obscure.

Leveraging your networks is not just about making connections; it is about nurturing relationships. Make an effort to grow your network both vertically and horizontally. Vertical network expansion connects you with experienced mentors, industry leaders, and influential personalities. These individuals hold the power of experience; they've been on the journey before, they can anticipate the obstacles you may stumble upon and guide you through them.

Speaking about mentors, do not underestimate the power of their wisdom. A mentor can hold a mirror up to you, helping you understand your strengths and exposing areas needing development. They can help you see things from a new perspective and often provide a guiding hand through complex business challenges.

Networking horizontally, on the other hand, puts you in touch with fellow entrepreneurs, perhaps even encountering the same issues as you. Engage in entrepreneurial communities -- both online and offline. Sharing experiences and knowledge with people in the same boat as you are encourages a sense of solidarity and provides an opportunity to learn from others' mistakes and successes.

Your team is another priceless resource. Trusted team members who share your vision can provide invaluable support and insight. Remember, diversity is a strength – it breeds creativity. Encourage your team to think freely and voice their opinions. A groundbreaking solution can come from the most unexpected quarters.

In addition to your internal resources, consider seeking external assistance. Business coaches, consultants, and industry specialists are an underutilized asset. They don't just offer expert advice but provide an outsider's perspective, critical and objective – helping you see the blindspots that you might have become oblivious to.

Additionally, financial advisors and legal consultants can guide you through complex aspects of business operations – from taxes and investments to regulations and legal issues.

Lastly, remember that being an entrepreneur is mentally taxing – busy schedules, high-stake decisions, constant pressure. It's okay to seek help from mental health specialists, like psychologists or therapists. They can provide strategies to manage stress and maintain your mental edge, enhancing your performance and decision-making abilities.

Leveraging your resources and networks is about building a strong nest of support that you can rely on when the winds get rough. Relationships, knowledge, diverse perspectives, and professional expertise are your true wealth as an entrepreneur, helping you navigate the choppy waters and sail towards success. Embrace these, and your entrepreneurial journey will not just be easier, but also enriching.

Fail Forward – Embrace Failure

Successful entrepreneurs practicing 'business with guts' share an unconventional appreciation for failure — they believe in the philosophy of failing forward. For them, defeat doesn't equate to a knockout, but instead, it marks the starting point of a new journey—the formation of an enriched game plan.

The traditional viewpoint on failure paints a negative, fatal picture. However, this new approach shifts the entire perspective on setbacks. Failing forward encourages you to use failure as a stepping-stone for success rather than a stumbling block.

Each setback isn't a barricade halting your progress, but a structured lesson providing insights about the direction that doesn't work. Real visionaries understand that every failure offers a wealth of wisdom. Regard it as a masterclass providing crucial insights into what doesn't work, equipping you with the knowledge of what could be done differently next time.

Decoding failure is not about reinvestigating slip-ups but about acknowledging that every misstep has an embedded code to decode, a one that unfurls a vital clue to refine your strategy. It's a process of continually adapting and learning. Take Thomas Edison, for example, who made 1,000 unsuccessful attempts before inventing the light bulb. When asked about his failures, he insightfully responded, "I didn't fail 1,000 times. The light bulb was an invention with 1,000 steps."

Hence, one big part of failing forward is about leveraging failure in your favor. A single defeat shouldn't mark the end—for every setback encountered, there are countless victories to be experienced.

The strength of a businessman with guts lies in resiliency and grit—an ability to pick oneself up, dust oneself off, and pivot when necessary. It is about sheer determination to jump back on the saddle after every fall, armed with fresh knowledge and stronger resolve. Each stumble makes you tougher, each bounce back makes you smarter, and each pivot drives you towards your goal with a sharper focus.

The process is often daunting, and it may even

invite skepticism or criticism. Yet, remember this—only when you withstand the storm can you appreciate the tranquility that follows. Those who are bold enough to embrace their failures, learn from them, and rise back up are the ones who ultimately edge past the finish line in the race to success.

So, opt to embrace failure—fail forward, learn, grow, and inch closer to your dream with each step. As the golden adage goes, it is always the darkest before dawn. Thus, endure the darkness and look forward to the inevitable sunrise—the dawn of your success.

In Summary

Undeniably, every entrepreneur who set out to change the world faced adversity. But it was their approach to these challenges that allowed them to make history.

Navigating challenges and setbacks is not about avoiding them but about handling them with courage, proactiveness, resilience, and keen learning. It relies on your ability to mould your mindset, leverage your networks and resources, learn from your failures, and keep an open mind for new opportunities.

So, the next time you're faced with an obstacle, embrace it. Stare it down, and boldly declare, "I saw you coming." Then, tackle it head-on. Remember, doing business with guts is not about playing safe, but about playing smart and brave. And sometimes, the greatest victories come after the hardest battles — it's time you fight yours!

8 INNOVATION AND CREATIVITY IN BUSINESS: BOLDLY SHAPING THE FUTURE WITH VISIONARY IDEAS

The canvas of business is constantly morphing, giving birth to new methodologies, technologies, and solutions. Among these disruptive elements, innovation and creativity remain the two cardinal points from which wealth creation happens. As fearlessly daring entrepreneurs, recognizing and fostering these twin elements can equip you to be a force de majeure in business — a force that disrupts the status quo, thinks outside the box, and shapes an astounding future.

Why Innovation?

To comprehend the magnitude of innovation's impact and the pivotal role it plays in business, one must first grasp its inherent trait of boundaryless existence. When you plunge into the pool of innovation, you immerse in a fluid world where boundaries separating different fields, different ideas, and even different realities start to blur. This boundless environment that innovation provides becomes a petri dish for new and exciting ideas to flourish and evolve.

The power of innovation does not stop at

presenting ideas. It amplifies the capacity to shake the intellectual pillars of accepted knowledge. It pushes against these pillars, tests their strength and durability, nudges them until they wobble, and eventually topple over. It shatters entrenched beliefs to pave the path for fresh ideas, encouraging diversity in thoughts and actions.

Moreover, innovation serves as a beacon, which lights up imaginative minds, ignites creativity, and sets the stage for ideation, cultivation, and maturation of vaunted concepts. Entrepreneurs, by accepting and fostering this blazing creativity, can ignite the wicks of their business dreams and witness them blast off to the highest realms of market presence and brand value.

Compellingly, innovation refuses to remain holed up in the realm of theory. It navigates beyond, pouring life into abstract ideas, crafting them into concrete solutions that leave trailblazing impact — solutions that not only surprise but inspire, not only disrupt but also reshape. As entrepreneurs, your ability to harness this innovative power, to fan its flames and mold its output, can generate an unparalleled value that distinguishes not only your business but your entrepreneurial identity.

Business giants, like Apple, Tesla, or Google, exemplify such entrepreneurial identities. Innovation is rooted deep within their corporate DNA. It was their undying spirit to tread along unchartered territories, combating the menacing shadows of the unknown, and their grit to mold nebulous ideas into tangible, awe-inspiring realities that propel them into the highest echelons of business success.

They didn't just create products; they wove entire realms of new experiences. Apple metamorphosed how we viewed phones, transforming them into extensions of our beings. Tesla dared to envision a future powered by sustainable energy and set afoot into the barely-explored electric vehicle industry. Google didn't just search; it molded the internet into an omnipresent, invaluable resource in our everyday lives. Simply put, these companies mimic the very essence of innovation, their history a testament to the endless possibilities it can unfold. And this is what etches them in the golden pages of corporate history.

The significance and the necessity of innovation, resoundingly clear, thus, remain non-negotiable in the business world's swiftly evolving landscape. To remain relevant, to leap ahead, and to survive, businesses now need to imbibe innovation and creativity at their very core.

Difference between Innovation and Invention

While both innovation and invention are quintessential elements of business growth and wealth creation, these terms significantly differ in their meanings and implications. A closer look at these concepts unveils the dynamics underscored by each one of them.

Invention: The Birth of Novelty

Invention is the physical manifestation of a novel idea or concept. It is the result of a unique realization that culminates in the creation of a product or a process that has never existed before. This unprecedented invention might take the form of a new gadget, a new methodology, a new algorithm or even a new formulation.

In essence, invention births the "new." It is the application of research, knowledge, and inventive thought to design and build something completely original. But being an invention doesn't automatically presuppose its market-fit, economic viability, or user acceptance. Some inventions may never even escape the prototype or patent stage.

Take, for example, Nikola Tesla's invention of alternating current. While it was a groundbreaking invention, it remained merely a scientific advancement until its mass usage was implemented, marking the birth of 'innovation.'

Innovation: The Actualization of an Idea

Innovation, juxtaposed to invention, is the process of implementing a new product or process into the commercial market effectively. It is about leveraging an invention or an existing idea to create value. This could manifest as satisfying unmet market needs, creating new markets, or altering business processes to boost efficiency and productivity.

Innovation is not just about grandiose, game-changing ideas but also about subtle improvements—an upgrade, a tweak, an enhancement—that can increase a product's value or applicability extensively. Moreover, innovation doesn't always hinge on a new invention; it could be a new, efficient way of using or repurposing an existing invention too.

The best example of this would be Apple's iPod which might not have been a fresh invention but was certainly a compelling innovation. This product repackaged existing technology (MP3 players were already in the market) and delivered it more effectively and appealingly to users.

In essence, every innovation might not be an invention, but every successful invention becomes an innovation when it hits the sweet spot of commercialization and societal impact. It's the innovative businesses that turn inventive ideas into tangible successes, effectively bridging the gap between a novel concept and commercial viability. Hence, as an entrepreneur, the challenge lies not only in creating or identifying a unique idea (invention) but also in reshaping and presenting it in a manner that solves a problem, meets a demand, and drives economic value (innovation).

Core Principles of Business Innovation

While innovation seems elusive, there's a science around cultivating it. The core crux comprises three elements: Cultivation, Disruption, and Iteration.

1. Cultivation: The seed of innovation resides in an atmosphere that promotes creativity, curiosity, and collaboration. Enterprises must encourage robust discussions, constructively critical thinking, and experimentation, thus cultivating a culture of innovation.

2. Disruption: A common misconception is that disruption is detrimental. However, in terms of innovation, disruption points to the ability to challenge the traditional and the accepted — it underlines having the nerve to disrupt your own business model before the market does.

3. Iteration: Innovation is not a one-time task, it's iterative. As the markets change, so do your customers' needs. Persistent reiteration, learning, and evolution are pivotal to stay relevant.

Creativity: The Lifeline of Business Innovation

Creativity acts as the heartbeat of innovation, a

primary life source that keeps the momentum of progress alive. This nurturing source is often overlooked, yet without it, innovation would essentially be a desolated landscape — an empty canvas with no colour or shape. Creativity is infused within every transformative concept, every novel system, and every paradigm shift. It collapses the fortifications of routine and monotony, bringing fervent beauty to the functional, rendering innovation a visible entity.

Creativity is an intangible element that constantly quivers beneath the surface of perceptive thinking. Entrepreneurs must delve deeper to tap into this reservoir. By relinquishing the tethering ropes of their comfort zones, they can dive into the realm of unrestrained imagination. This isn't an effortless leap; it calls for courage, audacity, and a true spirit of defiance.

Creativity occurs in that magical intersection

between the spontaneous ignition of a thought and its methodical realization. It thrives in a culture of openness, where there are no wrong ideas, where risk-taking is celebrated, and failures are treated as valuable teachers. However, the power of this formidable force truly manifests when creative energies are coupled with grit, discipline, and a tangible vision of their potential outcome.

To foster creativity, entrepreneurs must first demolish the mould of traditional frameworks and linear thinking. They must challenge long-standing norms, question accepted methodologies, and see beyond the predictable. By discarding the old guard, they invite novelty to take precedence and become prime drivers for innovative constructs.

This call for deconstruction, however, shouldn't imply a reckless dismantling of structures. Instead, denote it as a careful and conscious unsettling of rigidity, of the 'known', thus paving the way for unfettered thought processes. Once free from the constraints of conventional modes, organizations can initiate the metamorphosis into leaders of transformative innovation.

Creativity is more than flamboyance and artistic prowess. It expounds launch narratives spun from curiosity, defying conventional logic in quest of the unique. It's about harnessing innovative strategies and making calculated aberrations from the norm to serve the common yet unexpected needs. It involves exploratory missions into the terrains of industries, human psychology, and societal patterns, spotting connections where others see chasms.

Ultimately, entrepreneurs are the artists and their businesses the canvas — an ever-evolving masterpiece where creativity sows the seeds of innovation, making for real-life portraits of the bold, the fearful, the ambitious, and the prosperous. The creators of the business world who dare to be different, who feed from the wells of creativity, and forge ahead with confidence, literally imbibe the essence of the axiom - 'Business with Guts'.

Benefits of Innovation and Creativity

Entrepreneurs who consciously foster a culture of innovation and creativity in their businesses will reap transformative benefits.

1. Competitive Advantage: Nothing spells death for a business faster than stagnation. By injecting innovative ideas and creative solutions, a business remains dynamic and can stay ahead amidst fierce competition.

2. Customer Centricity: Innovation, coupled with creativity, opens doors for enhanced customer experience. It allows businesses to cater to their customers' evolving needs ingeniously and uniquely.

3. Revenue Growth: Innovative brands captivate customers. By drawing more patrons, they drive significant revenue growth.

4. Talent Attraction and Retention: Talented individuals are attracted to innovative companies. The promise of a challenging, creative environment becomes an irresistible magnet.

Boldly Shaping the Future with Visionary Ideas

The future of business rests on the audacious shoulders of innovation and creativity. Not only do they contribute to wealth creation, but they also help in building a legacy - a business that crafts its own unique narrative in the annals of history. The corporate future will belong to those daring entrepreneurs who believe their wildest, visionary ideas have the potential to reshape the world.

There is no play-safe avenue for towering business success. Audacity, innovation, creativity, risk – these have crafted the Billion-dollar business histories. So entrepreneur, do you have the guts to innovate and create the future?

In conclusion, harnessing the power of innovation and creativity is not just about being different; it's about making a difference. As you charge towards your success, remember, your ideas can change the world. So make them bold, make them creative, make them innovative and shape your entrepreneurial legacy because every start-up requires one essential element - Business with Guts.

9 BUILDING A SUSTAINABLE BUSINESS: BOLDLY MAKING A DIFFERENCE FOR GENERATIONS TO COME

Someone wise once opined, "Boldness be my friend". In the realm of business, boldness isn't just your friend—it's your essential ally. It is what transforms an idea into a reality, a vision into a thriving venture. But boldness isn't just about audacious actions and capitalizing on opportunity. It's also about sustainable strategies that endure turbulent times and succeed for generations, a notion we delve into in this chapter.

The pillars of a sustainable business, contrary to some misunderstood concepts, are not merely limited to eco-friendly operations. It encapsulates a visionary approach, diligence, innovation, resilience, and a firm commitment to making a positive impact, both socially and environmentally.

Visionary Approach: The first ball to juggle as an entrepreneur is developing a clear, long-term vision. It may be tempting to focus on the immediate market and quick profits, but remember that sustainable success favors the farsighted. Do not just aim to build a business; instead, create a legacy that will outlive you. Find the intersection between profitability and societal contribution, and you'll build a perpetual enterprise that transcends generations.

Diligence: No business can survive on the back of reckless decisions or blind luck. It demands diligence, meticulous planning, and constant review. Study market trends, understand your competition, listen to your customers, and consistently refine your strategies. The devil indeed is in the details. In this changing landscape of global business, due diligence is the compass that leads to the treasure of sustainability.

Innovation: As the saying goes - innovate or die. Innovation isn't just about groundbreaking products or disruptive business models. It's also about pioneering workplace practices, reinventing customer services, and spearheading sustainable operations. It requires a skyline view that surveys the macro landscape and a microscope that sees what others overlook. Boldness blended with innovation can create a transcendental cocktail of business sustenance and success.

Resilience: Every entrepreneur will meet unexpected roadblocks, market crashes, and the occasional failure. The odds can be overwhelming, but remember that the essence of entrepreneurship is risk, and risk's constant companion is failure. However, resilience turns these failures into gateways of growth. Embrace failure not as the end, but as a steppingstone towards success. Like a phoenix's rebirth from the ashes, rise with an invigorated spirit and the lessons from your disappointments.

Making a Difference: The final pillar of building a sustainable business rests on the ethos of your enterprise. Remember, your responsibility extends not only to your shareholders but also to the communities you serve. Develop business strategies that are organically intertwined with the welfare of the society and the environment around you. A business that earns respect will also earn revenue.

As an entrepreneur, your actions can spur an era of unprecedented growth and innovation for future generations. Build a culture that values sustainability, while also promoting entrepreneurial courage. Encourage your team to take smart risks and reward innovative failures. Foster a spirit of positive competition and build a culture that reveres the purpose beyond profits.

Brace for turbulence and remember, the road to sustainability is not a highway filled with roses, but a rough path that often requires you to reinvent the wheel. But don't falter. Be prepared to take mindful risks, defy the norms, and push the boundaries. After all, as a bold entrepreneur, your mission is not just to survive, but to flourish and create a legacy that future generations will hail as a lighthouse of business sustainability.

By fostering this brand of boldness, you won't merely become the talk of the town; you'll become the flourishing tree, providing shade to countless generations to come. It is all about changing the outlook from 'Business with Profits' to 'Business with Purpose'. That, my bold friend, is the crux of building a sustainable business that makes a difference for generations to come. It's about doing business with guts—without losing sight of your heart.

10 LEADING WITH PURPOSE - BOLDLY CREATING A LEGACY THAT MATTERS

In the rigorous and rousing world of entrepreneurship, "Business with Guts" isn't merely about accumulating wealth, but creating a legacy that mirrors audacity and purpose. It's about managing an entrepreneurial venture that's grounded in principles and powered by courage under fire, thus setting the stage for a ripple effect of lasting impact.

As a meaningful entrepreneur, leading with purpose isn't an option but an essentiality. This sort of leadership not only imprints an indelible societal impact, but is a game changer, rousing success and wealth in its wake. It's a story of those who dare deeply, act decisively, and influence intensely.

To translate such audacious leadership into actionable insights, we must dig deeper into three fundamental realms of purpose-driven leadership - Bold Vision, Resilient Execution, and Profound Impact.

1. Bold Vision: The Foundation of Audacity

The vision is the heart of entrepreneurial

leadership. A bold vision crystallizes a journey brimming with uncertainties, trials, and triumphs into a clear, compelling path. It's far more than just a mental pursuit; it's an emotional catalyst that drives persistence, discipline, and daring actions. It symbolizes the purpose, passion, and promise that an entrepreneurial venture holds. But laying the cornerstone of a bold vision involves reflective thinking, rigorous research, and, more importantly, radical courage. Learn to crystalize your visions, align them according to societal needs, and be audacious enough to give it an authentic voice.

2. Resilient Execution: Making Purpose a Performance

While a vision symbolizes the intent of an entrepreneurial venture, its execution reveals its identity. It's the performance that validates the promise of purpose-driven leadership. Resilient execution couples creativity with tenacity. It bridges the gap between ambitious ideas and astounding realities, making innovation an everyday phenomenon rather than a sporadic success. It traverses through unpredictable economic landscapes, remains unwavered by daunting challenges, preserves an unyielding commitment to the vision, and, above all, takes giant strides with grit and grace.

3. Profound Impact: The Legacy That Matters

The long-lasting legacies aren't just about profits and power. They are the byproduct of audacious endeavors that alter the course of economies, societies, and lives. An entrepreneurial venture that stands the test of time and strives beyond the bottom line success leaves a legacy that matters. It's not just about creating value but about proliferating values. As you articulate the purpose and define the course, let your entrepreneurial journey create ripples of impact leading towards an ocean of changes. The essence of profound impact lies in dancing at the edges of audacity, awakening change, and inspiring future generations.

Remember, leading with purpose is about cultivating a business terrain where fortunes thrive alongside principles, and ambitions align with actions.

Don't merely aim to be the best in the world; strive to be the best for the world. This audacious entrepreneurial journey might demand sacrifices, struggle, and sweat. It might shake you to your core but will leave you with a legacy that truly matters.

Ventures blooming with purpose are the ones that bear sweet fruits of economic prosperity and societal wellbeing. They are a beacon of bravery -

illuminating a path for others to follow, becoming a testament to audacious dreams and dogged determination.

The baton of bold leadership is in your hands. Now, it's up to you to forge new paths, build bridges of impact, and lead with purpose to create a legacy that remains in the annals of entrepreneurial history, long after the final profits have been tallied.

Stay audacious, stay visionary, and cultivate a business with guts. That's how you create a legacy that matters; that's how you cultivate a life well-lived.

CONCLUSION

In any story of triumph, there are mishaps and lost battles. The same is true in the world of entrepreneurship. From our journey here in "Business with Guts", we have tackled impromptu risks, stinging reluctance, the courage of bold decisions, and the sheer audacity of dreams. The secret to business success and wealth was never meant to be simple or easy, rather it is meant to test our fortitude and tenacity. So as we cap this interesting exploration, let's revisit our key takeaways and put the final pieces of this paradoxical puzzle together.

Firstly, risk-taking is not about jumping into the fire blindly. It's about informed decisions and calculated risks. Running a business, after all, is not gambling; it's a strategic game of chess where knowing when and what to move is of utmost importance. You'll need to be both a discerning decision-maker and a risk-taker when the situation calls.

For every calculated risk you take, remember that it comes with its own erratic set of possibilities which could either pave the way to success or redirect you to another route. The determination to pursue a particular course of action despite potential adversity lies in having guts. A willingness to fail, coupled with an indomitable spirit is what separates the might-have-beens from the legends.

In addition, reluctance is a normal human instinct that tends to prevail when we stare into the unknown. But to make the grade in business, whether you're a greenhorn entrepreneur or a seasoned business magnate, you must be receptive to stepping out of your comfort zone. Reluctance has no place in a mind conditioned for success. It stems from fear, and as we've discussed throughout this book, fear can either cripple you or drive you towards breakthroughs.

Moreover, the entrepreneurial world is not for the meek. It calls for bold decisions where hesitation is a ground lost. Your actions should be dictated by conviction, not apprehension. There will be days when you feel like Sisyphus, condemned to push a boulder up a hill, only for it to roll back down. The beautiful part is the rising sun of a new day, offering a new chance, a chance to push again.

Lastly, having guts in business is about the audacity to dream: to visualize success, and to have an unwavering belief in these dreams. Entrepreneurship is often characterized by rollercoaster-like ups and downs. Your dreams become your north star, an anchor amidst a raging sea, guiding you towards the uncharted territories of success. To dream is to envision a future where you're standing on the mountaintop, basking in the fruits of your labor and perseverance.

Now, as we descend from this mountaintop view of business with guts, remember that each chapter touched on a crucial aspect of entrepreneurship and courage. We've highlighted the importance of being bold and not letting fear drive. We've learned to honor the power of calculated risks and befriend failure. This buoyant spirit is what sets you apart in the dog-eat-dog world of business.

And as you close this book, remember that the journey doesn't end here. The lessons you've learned are meant to be applied, absorbed, and passed on. Spread the knowledge so that others might also strive to be bolder, braver entrepreneurs.

Success in business is never a solo enterprise. To those around you, be the leader who empowers others. Be the mentor who nurtures their growth – impart upon them the courage to reach for their dreams, to be mavericks with a vision, who look past the challenges and into the vast emptiness of the unknown with a determined smile.

This is where our story ends – with a challenge. A challenge to you, to supersede the conventional. To ignite within yourself the blazing spirit of audacious entrepreneurship. To stand tall with an unyielding resolve to be not just a player, but a game-changer. A titan in the world of business.

"Business with Guts" has never been just a title, but a rallying cry for all entrepreneurial spirits to rise and thrive in. It's a testament that captures the essence of running a business – it's daring, tough, filled with uncertainty, yet incredibly rewarding.

Remember, the world of entrepreneurship doesn't need followers…it needs leaders with guts. Your business journey has been, is, and will forever be a testament to your courage. Wear it like a badge of honor. You went beyond dreaming…you dared to actualize and for that, you've made all the difference.

Here's to your unraveled courage and future business success. Welcome to the world of doing "Business with Guts".

ABOUT THE AUTHOR

Author Senton Kaçaniku is a renowned entrepreneur, commercial lawyer and sought-after business consultant. A postgraduate of Salford Business School, Senton has pursued a corporate, startup and political journey that has been nothing less than inspirational. With over 15 years of business experience, he has founded and led countless startups and turned struggling businesses into profitable ventures.

Having worn various hats from being a passionate visionary to a meticulous CEO, Senton has tested the waters of risk and reward and understands deeply what it means to run a business with 'guts'. He firmly believes that audacious endeavors and smart risks are the backbone of any business achievement, and this belief serve as the foundation of his strategies.

Senton is not just a successful entrepreneur but also a philanthropist, investing in ideas and people around the world. This book is his attempt to share his insights and lessons gained from his many entrepreneurial adventures. He wishes to inspire the next generation of entrepreneurs to be fearless in their pursuit of success. He splits his time between the United States, Europe, the Middle East and Africa, enjoying the excitement of building businesses which span across continents.

Printed in Great Britain
by Amazon